Starting Life

Frog

Claire Llewellyn
illustrated by Simon Mendez

It is an April morning, and a frog has just laid her eggs in a pond. It took her a while because she laid so many—about 4,000 eggs in all.

Perch

Frogspawn makes a mass of jelly that is hard for animals to attack.

A frog's eggs are called frogspawn. Each egg looks like a tiny, black dot, wrapped up in a blob of jelly. The jelly helps to protect the egg from dangers in the pond.

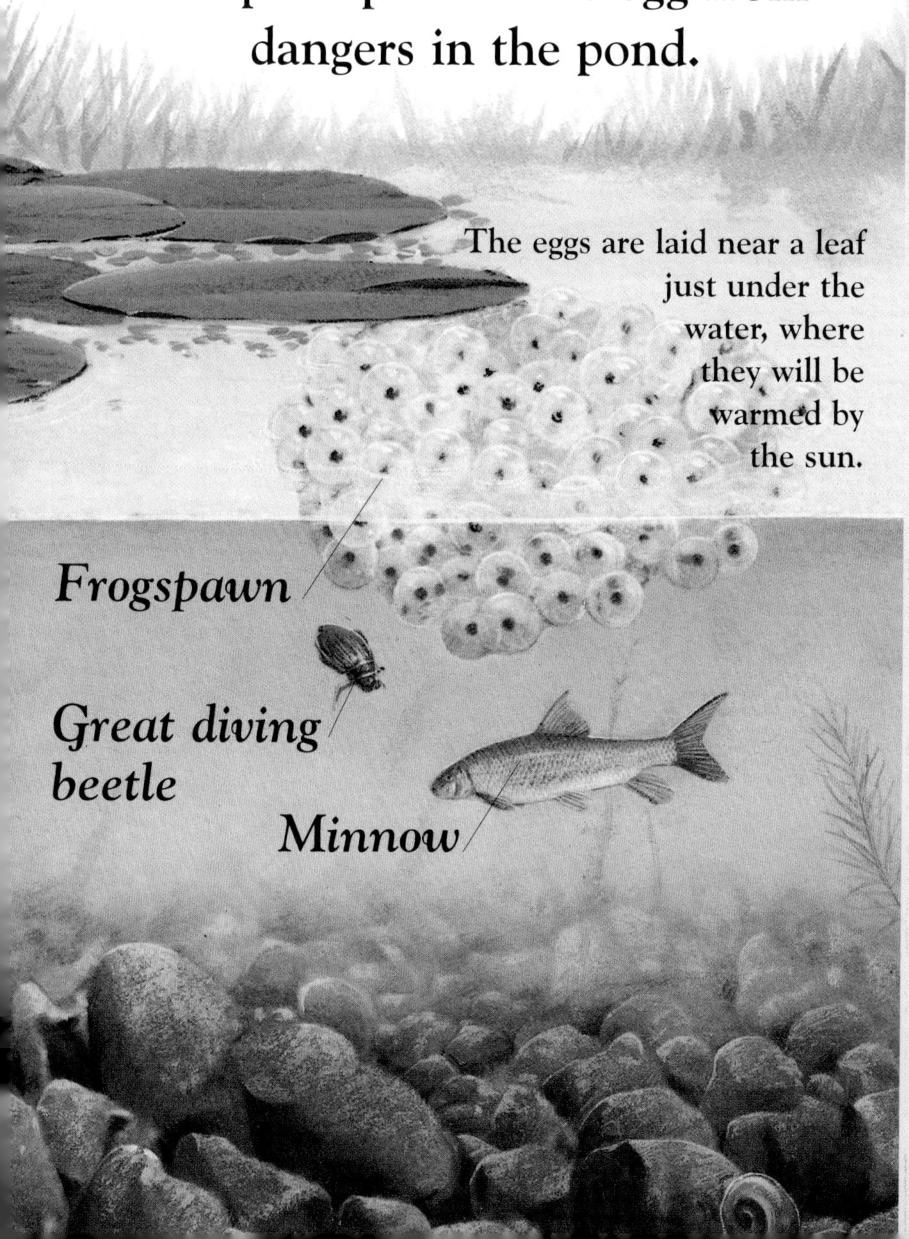

The eggs are laid near a leaf just under the water, where they will be warmed by the sun.

Frogspawn

Great diving beetle

Minnow

The eggs quickly begin to change. Day by day embryos develop inside the eggs and soon they start to look like tadpoles. Two weeks later they begin to hatch.

Lily pad

A new tadpole has a sticky patch on its belly to help it cling to underwater plants.

The egg hatches

Newly-hatched tadpoles are not ready to swim. They cling to the jelly and underwater leaves and stems as they develop for a few days more.

An embryo develops inside each egg. This is the beginning of a tiny tadpole.

About two weeks after the eggs were laid, the tadpoles hatch into the water.

Water snail

Three days later the tadpoles are swimming around the pond. The hundreds of tiny, black bodies wriggle their tails to power them through the water.

Tadpoles have many enemies. Dragonfly larvae are fierce hunters that grab tadpoles in their jaws.

Tadpoles feed on the slimy water plants called algae that grow on underwater stones and leaves.

Dragonfly larva

The pond is a dangerous place for tadpoles. Many of them end up as meals for fish, newts, dragonfly larvae, and big, black diving beetles.

Tadpoles grow black, feathery gills on their heads. Gills help tadpoles to breathe in water.

Long, strong tail

Rounded head

Diving beetle larva

Just two weeks after hatching out of the egg, the tadpoles start to change. First their tails get longer. Then back legs begin to grow.

Water lily in bud

Water spider

Every day the tadpoles' gills grow smaller. Soon they will disappear.

Meanwhile, inside their tiny bodies, lungs are beginning to develop. These will soon take the place of the gills and allow the tadpoles to breathe air.

A tadpole sprouts a pair of back legs. Each leg grows five long toes.

Over the next few weeks, the tadpoles grow a pair of front legs and their gills completely disappear. Now the animals swim to the surface to fill their lungs with air.

As the legs grow bigger and the tail grows shorter, the tadpoles look more like frogs.

Froglet

With their bulgy eyes, wide mouths, and broadening bodies, the tadpoles look more like frogs. They are called froglets now. This amazing change from a tadpole to a frog is known as metamorphosis.

Yellow iris

By midsummer there are fewer tadpoles in the pond. Many have been eaten by predators.

Four weeks after the back legs appeared, the front legs start to sprout.

Week by week, the froglets grow bigger and stronger. Now, in the last warm days of summer, they begin to leave the pond. Frogs belong to a group of animals called amphibians. Amphibians begin their lives in water, but as adults they live on land.

The tail is taken in by the body. It grows smaller every day.

Water lily

Water lilies grow on long, rubbery stems that are rooted in the bottom of the pond.

The froglet's body is still changing. The little, stubby tail is beginning to shrink. Soon, the tail will disappear. There is also something growing inside the mouth. It is the frog's long, sticky tongue!

Young frogs crawl out of the water, but they stay very near the pond.

About two years after leaving the pond, a frog is fully grown. By now it is three or four inches (8-10 cm) long with greenish-brown, speckled skin. A frog has very big, bulging eyes. Behind each eye is an eardrum called the tympanum, which helps the frog pick up sounds.

Smooth, damp skin

Female frog

Frogs are small, but they can leap surprisingly far. By pushing against their strong back legs, they cover a lot of ground. Frogs move well in water, too. Their long, webbed feet make perfect flippers and help them to be strong swimmers.

The typanum, or eardrum, is the dark circle on the side of the frog's head. These are bigger on male frogs than on the females.

Male frog

A frog's front legs are very short. It uses them to prop itself up when it is sitting on the ground.

A frog is not a fussy eater and feeds on many kinds of food. It darts out of the water to gulp down snails and grab flies that buzz through the air. On land it hunts for grasshoppers, spiders, beetles, worms, and other kinds of insects.

Zap! A cricket is blasted by the sticky tip of the frog's long tongue.

At times a frog will sit quietly for hours, waiting for a meal to come by. When it does, the frog uses its deadly weapon—its long, fast, sticky tongue. The frog shoots the victim, reels it back in, then swallows it down in a gulp.

A frog's big eyes are on the side of its head so that it can see all around.

So many animals feed on frogs that they have a hard job staying alive. Otters, fish, birds, and snakes are excellent frog-hunters.

Bittern

A sharp-eyed heron pounces with its long, pointed beak and plucks a frog out of the water.

A frog's speckled skin makes it hard to see. This way of hiding against the background is known as camouflage.

Pike

Luckily, frogs have a number of defenses that help to protect them. As long as they keep still, frogs are very hard to see because the greenish-brown color of their skin matches their surroundings. Also, because of their eyes and excellent hearing, frogs are quick to sense danger.

Otter

A snake slithers along beside the pond waiting to catch an unlucky frog.

A frog leaps into the pond to escape from danger, but pike, perch, and other hunters are lurking in the depths.

The days are growing colder and winter is on the way. The frogs search for a safe place where they can find shelter. Young frogs and females hide on land, under logs or piles of leaves. Here, they fall into a deep winter sleep called hibernation.

Reeds die back in winter.

When a frog hibernates, its heart barely beats at all.

Adult males hibernate not on land but in the mud at the bottom of the pond. Instead of breathing through their lungs, they breathe very slowly through their skin. At times the pond freezes over, but so long as there is water at the bottom of the pond, the sleeping frogs will survive.

Fish rest in the deepest part of the pond. As the water cools, they also slow down. Fish feed very little during the winter, so the frogs can hibernate in safety.

The bed of the pond is covered with soft mud and rotting leaves. It's a good place for frogs to hibernate.

The cold months pass, and it is early spring. Now, as the days grow longer and warmer, the frogs begin to stir. The males swim up to the surface of the pond and the females also wake from hibernation. Still sleepy, the females slowly make their way towards the pond.

New eggs

One bright, spring morning a loud croaking fills the air. At the pond, the male frogs are calling to the females, who soon come and join them to breed. Soon a new mass of frogspawn floats in the water, and new frogs start life in the pond.

Algae begin to grow in the water. They will provide food for the tadpoles when they hatch.

A pond is a busy place in spring. Frogs, fish, newts, and other creatures lay their eggs in the warming water.

A male frog's call sounds like a CROAK! It attracts females to the pond. A group of calling males can be very loud.

Glossary and Index

Algae (AL-jee) Small plants that grow as a covering on rocks and plants under water. 6, 23

Amphibian (am-FIH-bee-un) A group of animals, including frogs, toads, newts and salamanders, that live partly in freshwater and partly on land. They mostly lay their eggs in water. 12

Camouflage (KAM-uh-flaj) The colors and markings on an animal that help it to blend in with its surroundings and make it difficult to see. 18

Eardrum A thin, circular piece of skin that picks up sound. 15

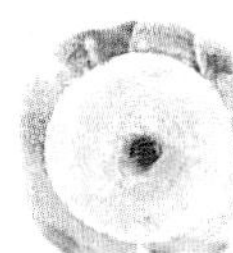

Embryo (EM-bree-oh) The tiny, living creature that develops from an animal's egg. 4, 5

Froglet The stage between a tadpole and a frog. 11, 12, 13

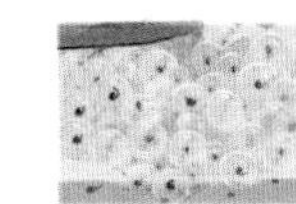

Frogspawn A mass of frog's eggs wrapped up in jelly. 2, 3, 23

Gills The part of the body on an amphibian or fish that helps it to breathe under water. 7, 8, 9

Hibernation (hi-ber-NAY-shun) A long, deep sleep that helps animals to survive the winter. 20, 21, 22